ONLY THIS BLUE

A LONG POEM

WITH AN ESSAY

BETSY WARLAND

THE MERCURY PRESS

The publisher gratefully acknowledges the financial assistance of the
Canada Council for the Arts, the Ontario Arts Council, and the Ontario
Book Publishing Tax Credit Program. The publisher further acknowledges
the financial support of the Government of Canada through the
Department of Canadian Heritage's Book Publishing Industry
Development Program (BPIDP) for our publishing activities.

Some of these poems have appeared in *CV2*; the essay, "Nose to Nose,"
was first published in *The Capilano Review*.

Poetry editor: Beverley Daurio
Editor for the press: Rachel Zolf
Cover design and composition: Beverley Daurio
Cover photograph: Cheryl Sourkes and Betsy Warland
Dedication: with gratitude to my teacher, Joanne Broatch

Printed and bound in Canada
Printed on acid-free paper

1 2 3 4 5   09 08 07 06 05

Library and Archives Canada Cataloguing in Publication
Warland, Betsy, 1946-
        Only this blue / Betsy Warland.
Poems. ISBN 1-55128-118-X
        I. Title.
PS8595.A7745O5 2005   C811'.54   C2005-905297-X

The Mercury Press
Box 672, Station P   Toronto, Ontario Canada M5S 2Y4
www.themercurypress.ca

ONLY THIS BLUE

ONLY THIS BLUE

resolution on the small black & white screen
is poor
      in the darkened room
she makes writing motions on my skin
searches for density & shape

                    – angle is everything –

      i suggest i stand

touching the image next to me, she says

That's your bowel.

interior motion roiling boil
of normalcy
             layers of
muscle   grain of wood   current of water

the mirror

the brush

            , daily
in & out
of my hands like water

i had ceased noticing
their shapes on the shelf

this forgetting cannot
observe itself
            is quick
                  with

necessity

– learning green –

contemplation of cold buds
poised through winter
seeds bulbs roots wrapped in
endless earth night

i have taken to wearing

green

my hairless head a shy
perseverant shoot

two days away
alone
i happen upon words
carved in a side table:

Plant your seeds deeply...
and look into the darkness.

amidst all this earnest green

pink   of
        shower   petals

boy
        tossing soccer ball

                        blue-sky ward

language of green ever in between

bud & bough   earth & sky

who could ever speak

green?

on the sidewalk my steps
   cushioned by cherry blossoms

         on either side
   pink
                  -studded grass

shouting   punches   fragrant
morning air

        three figures run
     with white bag

i slip behind
yellow van

down the laneway
the tallest man stops

inching my head out

     – points of his eyes –

fix on mine
    air tense

   the other two sprint across yards

yell

— breath a fist —

i step
back into laneway
my son needs milk

near the corner store
on tender grass
a rifle

startling as a body

she tells of her kids
in the backseat
wanting to see where she
                    grew up

the address was right but
the house torn down
    , creek filled in
hill gone

the body wants to recognize itself

seeks reassurance even in
familiar flaws

        reflective surfaces are everywhere

        _____

        someone else looks back

what we call perception
is mostly habit

just well enough to run for the bus
i move with surprising exuberance
unusual ease

                    – then body recalls itself –

this is me
before
i had breasts

slope of day diminishes
as tide of night slips in

at the top of the top-most tree
robin thinks of nothing but to sing
light out, sing
dark in

its variant double-notes gather us each to all
bridging entente
enfolding & unfolding
as the

night as the day
as our
arms around one another

i flail
      in a sea of   newgreen

gust upon gust

body
      buffeted
            by sound
              assault

i myself an unknown season

a-rhythmical
                , differently
balanced

with things cut out
                                    & off
  &
        things put in

things
        thin-bare
        tight
wane

things
stitched together

, falling out

unspeakable sensations

of never the same

the body cowers
in bone-thinness   despite
              nascent fluidity of
                   dappled light

                                   avoids

newleaf
shadows
suddenly
clotting sidewalks

(spectral chill)

              – ink into blotter –

– daystar embrace –

then there's skin of sky

    & how it incites leaves

       to stroke it

will you, green?

i lie next
to these poems

i lie
next to you

       , intimacy   contingent

in the mail
a red hat

       just as her stubble hinted
at flourishing
            red
slips out of manila envelope
                            out
of purple wrapping paper   & the
                      green-raw
silk on her head
           yelps

           wants to chase, catch its tail

she suspected
a delicately thin layer of latex
seduced
touch
        away from implication

three days after surgery, she
draws back the syringe

            – syringe, gloves –

hadn't expected to find these
in the cartridge-refill kit

beginning the procedure

        – sensation of smooth remove –

                                        hitting
fast as general anaesthetic

she observes an opaque fog
enveloping everything except

    – the site –

body
chilling
    with detachment

pathology of oil by-products

        – the Romans and their lead –

cultures
of breast-cancer cells
      discovered
to rapidly multiply

in plastic Petri dishes

decision:

> what is familiar
> what is preferred
> what is expected
> what is calculated
> what is efficient
> what is gratifying

& what of the decision
no one
wants to make?

> — Pilate washing his hands —

protocol, statistics
herding our terror
evading questions
dodging contradiction

she asked for a dream
awoke on its smooth edge

     – knife hovering in luminous space –

a kitchen knife, unremarkable
except for cedar-green handle

    hours later
waiting for the light to change
she gets   the yes of green

level with her breasts   , the knife
not floating but

              calmly offered

in her red
dictionary months later
        a word catches her eye

    decide, dē-, off + *cadere*

                to cut

red continued to astonish

                    – maple's red halo –

though each bud remains tight-
lipped at its tip
                    red filaments tentacle the sky

                    – tidal pool of red anemones –

maple's seven kinds of strength –
one spoken:

The red precedes the green.

                    how she knew
to accept   red syringed into blue vein
                            of her hand

three white-lab-coat dreams
the fourth, a radiant bald woman
in three-quarter-length red coat
strides
        out of the elevator

in her waking
crow
      caws
           at

                  – muscularity of green –

how
blade & leaf
assume the spaces

at café window seat:
       You're lucky.
       By the time they found out,
       it was too late for my dad

                         – behind glass –

red-buoyant tow truck pulls
tilted black hearse

prognostic pilgrimage

        – enveloped by ancient red –

hiking down Grand Canyon

      how our skins softly greened

the course?

    water plummets

        − not knowing, not knowing −

      , she stands
              on viewing platform
not knowing, not
knowing

camera expects a casual pose
insisting sameness
in every situation

inside the viewfinder
a green & red light
inform photographer
whether subject

is in or out
of focus

     through the past three seasons   she

     absent
     from rectangled story

                      , now

     – goes through the motions –

        body porous as water   air   leaf

two hundred and eleven feet
two hundred and eleven feet, two
hundred and eleven
feet, two hundred and eleven feet

– plunge –

the shape

the weight

water

makes

arrowing from

earth to

earth

– migratory flight pattern –

scales of fish
    wake, wedge
        caveat, cleavage
            pubis of

– pulling off yellow turtleneck –

last threads break
       of Buddhist protection-cord prayer

– red encircled my neck –

for fifteen months staying

my
fear

yellow   punctures the glee

give   grandstand of green

asserts:
no exit
yield
slow for curve
merge
mind the steps
do not cross over

      the   prickly   rain

               new

pelt of green

     – yellow bulldozer poised –

outside my studio window

      tough brown oak leaves
murmured monkish sutras
                  all winter 'til March
    gusts
        shoo them from

               branch-bud rows
                    && rows

of sitting cushions

oak last to be coaxed

    ignores variable sky's   ice-blue

        awaits
        warmthrough before

                    – assenting squint –

   yellowyellow-green novitiates
settle in

  adjust their robes

greed & grace & gulp of green

flashing signature of

                        yellow-headed

yellow-bellied

                                 yellow-throated

yellow-legged

                yellow-footed

            yellow-eyed

                             yellow-breasted

                yellow-rumped

Hello!

– to dare yellow –

, pulling it up by its roots
or poisoning it
            yell, Oh!

                        scars of what has been

– aperture of yellow –

(come close)

the cloudless solitude of knowing

when knowing has not been
                              evidenced

how a single word can stalk you
for seven years, hurl itself

            – out of the blue –

from bookshelves, newsstands

with the certain grace of a planet

an oval stone
          revolves end over end
toward your forehead

slow-motion
you observe
its approach
          hands shuttering face

          as it cracks the windshield

to not be afraid when there was
every reason to fear

understanding tethered to
not wanting to know

blue observes all colours

reflects all colours

hearts the flame

ocean-soft summer twilight
on seawall promenade

an astronomer
                sets up his telescope
invites viewers

            one taker
                        – particularly enthralled –

            calls through azure darkening:

                Come see the moon. It's free!

Come see the moon –

it's *free*!

to not be afraid when
there is every reason to fear

                  – we know what we must do –

there is no outcome

                                only this blue

Nose to Nose

With the iambs of our infant breathing, rhythmic cycles of our bodily functions, patterns of sound and motion within our domestic surroundings, repetitive song of our distinctive crying, and comforting melodies of our parents' voices, poetry embraces us into our being here.

The structure of poem is before, after, inside, and outside of words. We call it rhythm, rhyme, pattern, meter, cadence, tone. We call it the poem's musicality, form, impulse.

Poem is wave.

At poem's base is the depth of our unknowing. At its crest our knowing. In the movement between – poem's urgent momentum.

Because poem's very form acknowledges both what can be said or known and never said or known, poetry may be as close as we come through language to the sacred.

Lyric form is the lineage of poem, as it is of sacred and mystical texts.

Poems that prick our imagination from generation to generation structurally encounter the known and unknown: this is the lineage pulsing within us.

Poetry, as music, is intrinsically an airborne art form: poem must navigate page like a voice in space. Contemporary poetry often appears to be a visual art form, yet the most compelling poems integrate sound and sight.

When hearing poem in a language from a culture we do not know, full comprehension remains out of reach. Unlike prose, however, poem's signalling power is nevertheless operative. Poems transmit the sentiments of their sonic territories via each poem's unique set of emotive tones and narrative energy. We are impacted on a cellular level. Poem "speaks" to us in the same way that "foreign" music and visual art get through to us.

The body breathes the poem breathes the page.

When poem and the poet's body share a profound intimacy, poem and page become lovers — nose to nose — inhaling/exhaling one another's breath.

Scored spaces inhale.

                                Scored lines exhale.

Most inscribed systems we have devised to represent meaning — written language, science notation, sheet music, math, and a number of the visual arts — rely on a related progression of configured lines and spaces. In poetry, "blank" spaces and "inscribed" lines converge: have comparable entitlement.

Language evidences our separateness.

Silence evidences what we share.

Poem's uninscribed spaces may mean different things to different people, but these meanings do not need to be specified. We abide in them. The uninscribed space of the page is a powerful form of communication, as is silence: both are often mistaken for emptiness, excess, or being extrinsic.

Silence and space potentially hold all language and meaning.

Language acknowledges our separateness by insisting on telling us something specific. It is generated from our desire to connect, or to bridge a sensed gap in memory, perception, or feeling.

Poetry is a riptide where language and silence negotiate each other's equally powerful currents.

Ultimately, sound (language) and silence (scored space) are the same thing: emphasis and meaning.

Accurate scoring of poem is critical. If the inscribed poem remains faithful to the intonation, pausing, emphasis, and rhythm of its oral expression, then its meaning is vivified. As in a piece of music, accurate scoring enables readers to see, breathe and speak poem as it was composed, delivering readers soundly into their own interpretations.

The integrity of poem hinges on its set of specific circumstances. Just as a composer tends to write choral music to move through a cathedral's time and space, or a lullaby to move through domestic time and space, so the poet composes each poem. These circumstances invite us in; without them poem remains obscured, closed.

Within its particular time and space, poem is liberated to gesture toward, hint at. Is a sketch. A note. A brush stroke.

Poetry arouses us via devotion to articulating sensation, uncoiling perception – not by proof or explanation.

Poem is porous.

Scored pauses within poem create openings for anticipation, exchanged glances, and exclamation.

Scored stanza breaks allow time for the reader's recognition of her or his own associations, thoughts.

Poem is a field of molecular word activity. The poet senses what is *already there* and navigates accordingly. If we travail faithfully, we can return years later and be startled by poem's wisdom, insight, beauty – of which we were not fully cognizant before.

Poetry is change in the act of. Like beauty, its fluidity surprises and transforms us. As with species' survival, poem embodies resilient inventiveness.

Poem enters your heart the way idea enters your mind.

Although poetry has narrative elements, its instincts and lineage are distinct from prose narrative's instincts and lineage.

Prose takes us on a journey.

Poetry may be the journey.

OTHER BOOKS BY BETSY WARLAND

Bloodroot — Tracing the Untelling of Motherloss, 2000

What Holds Us Here, 1998

Two Women in a Birth (with Daphne Marlatt), 1994

The Bat Had Blue Eyes, 1993

Proper Deafinitions, 1990

Double Negative (with Daphne Marlatt), 1988

serpent (w)rite, 1987

open is broken, 1984

A Gathering Instinct, 1981